CW01262710

Original title:
The Sparkling Frost

Copyright © 2024 Swan Charm
All rights reserved.

Author: Paulina Pähkel
ISBN HARDBACK: 978-9908-1-1864-2
ISBN PAPERBACK: 978-9908-1-1865-9
ISBN EBOOK: 978-9908-1-1866-6

Crystal Prism of Cold

In the night where stars do play,
Snowflakes dance in bright array.
Colors burst in frosty air,
Laughter echoes everywhere.

Candles glow with warmest light,
Joyful hearts in pure delight.
Children's voices fill the streets,
Where winter's magic gently meets.

Icicles hang like jewels fair,
Sparkling gems both bright and rare.
Each breath forms a cloud of white,
A moment captured, pure as light.

Together we embrace the cheer,
As love and friendship draw us near.
In this world of crystal gleam,
We celebrate our warmest dream.

Frosty Embers of Dawn

Morning breaks with hues so bright,
Golden rays chase off the night.
Frosty embers warm the ground,
In this hush, new dreams are found.

Leaves, like diamonds, catch the sun,
Whispers of the day begun.
Breath of winter, crisp and clear,
Carols sung for all to hear.

Hot cocoa in our hands, we smile,
Sharing laughter all the while.
Footprints mark the snowy scene,
Together in this joyful dream.

Nature's beauty, pure and bright,
In the dawn's enchanting light.
Frosty air, a warm embrace,
In this wondrous, festive space.

Glimmering White Silence

Silent night, a world aglow,
Blankets white, like winter's show.
Stars above, they twinkle high,
In this peace, our spirits fly.

Snowflakes fall with gentle grace,
Each one unique, a fleeting trace.
Children play, their laughter rings,
In this hush, the heart takes wing.

Candles flicker with soft light,
Guiding souls through winter's night.
Whispers shared by fire's glow,
Memories cherished, hearts in tow.

Glimmers dance on frozen streams,
Woven stories, woven dreams.
In this white, serene embrace,
We find joy in every space.

Icy Latticework of Nature

Branches twine in frosty lace,
Nature's artwork takes its place.
Each sharp edge and crystal form,
Crafted by the winter's charm.

Whispers in the biting breeze,
Rustling leaves on frozen trees.
Underneath the moon so bright,
Magic lingers in the night.

Footprints crunch on snowy trails,
As laughter weaves through winter gales.
Gather round the fire's glow,
Tell the tales that make joy grow.

In this world of icy grace,
Love and warmth we all embrace.
Hand in hand, we laugh and sing,
Celebrating all that winter brings.

Hidden Frosted Treasures

Softly gleaming in the night,
Whispers of the frosty light.
Under stars that brightly dance,
Dreams awaken, hearts in trance.

Glistening paths to wander near,
Hidden treasures, joys we cheer.
Snowflakes twirl in joyful glee,
Nature's gift, so wild and free.

Candles flicker, warmth inside,
Laughter wraps us, joy our guide.
Frosted branches, shimmering bright,
Gather close, embrace the night.

Frost-Kissed Reverie

Morning mist with icy breath,
Nature wakes from winter's death.
Each breath a cloud, so soft and white,
Turning dreams to pure delight.

Frost-kissed trees, a magic scene,
Sparkling coats of silver sheen.
Children laughing, snowballs fly,
Underneath the vast, blue sky.

Joyful songs fill frosty air,
With each note, we shed our care.
Celebrate this day, we must,
In the frost, we place our trust.

Dazzling Frostfall

Dancing flakes, a swirling bliss,
Winter's grace, a tender kiss.
Icy breath upon the ground,
In this beauty, joy is found.

Children twirl in joyful spins,
Chasing laughter, where it begins.
Frostfall paints a world so bright,
Magic glows in pale moonlight.

Gather 'round the fire's embrace,
Tales of winter, love, and grace.
Hot cocoa warms our eager hands,
Dazzling joy in winter lands.

Iced Symphony

Notes of winter softly play,
An iced symphony today.
Chords of joy, all hearts do sing,
In this moment, life's a fling.

Nature's canvas, pure and bright,
Frosty tunes in morning light.
With each sparkle, dreams ignite,
Music swirls in pure delight.

Gather friends, let voices rise,
Underneath the starlit skies.
Together we will weave a tale,
In this frosty, joyful gale.

A Cascade of Glacial Light

Sparkling snowflakes dance in the night,
Joyful laughter echoes, hearts so light.
Colors glimmer under the moon's soft glow,
A cascade of dreams in the chilly snow.

Candles flicker, casting warm delight,
Families gather, spirits shining bright.
With every cheer, a spirit takes flight,
In this wondrous world, everything feels right.

Twilight's Icy Brush

Twilight whispers, a touch of grace,
The world wrapped in a frosty embrace.
Stars emerge from their silvery layer,
As snowflakes twirl in a festive prayer.

Children's giggles blend with the night,
As they chase shadows in pure delight.
The air vibrant, with joy intertwined,
In twilight's dance, our hearts are aligned.

Frost's Shining Whispers

Frosted trees gleam in the pale moonlight,
Nature's secrets, a sparkling sight.
Soft whispers of winter fill the air,
Each frosty branch a tale to share.

Joyful hearts pulse with the season's song,
In this winter wonder, we all belong.
With shared laughter and friends so dear,
The magic of frost draws us near.

Enchantment of the Frozen

In enchanted realms where the cold winds play,
The frozen world shimmers, bright as day.
With every sigh, the magic unfolds,
A tapestry woven in silver and gold.

Merriment crowns each frosty glance,
As we gather 'round, lost in the dance.
With hearts aglow and spirits embraced,
In the frozen night, our worries erased.

Gleaming Paths in a Silent Wonderland

Snowflakes dance through the air,
Children's laughter fills the night.
Stars above with a joyful glare,
Gathered warmth, hearts feeling light.

Lanterns glow with a gentle cheer,
Footprints trace the sparkling way.
Whispers of happiness draw near,
Winter's magic, here to stay.

The Brightness within Winter's Grip.

Fires crackle, shadows play bright,
Mittens hug hands in delight.
Cocoa sipped, marshmallows swirl,
In this season, joy unfurls.

Snowman smiles in the yard's embrace,
Joyful voices in a race.
Underneath the midnight sky,
Festive spirits soar up high.

Winter's Diamond Gleam

Icicles glimmer, a sparkling show,
Fields of white and the softest glow.
In each heart, a flame ignites,
Celebrations fill wondrous nights.

Carols sung with a joyful air,
Gifts wrapped neatly, moments to share.
As snowflakes whisper their soft refrain,
We cherish warmth in the cold's domain.

Crystals in the Moonlight

Moonbeams dance on fresh, white sheets,
Nature's diamond, a sight so sweet.
With every step, the world awakes,
Magic twinkles, joy it makes.

Families gather 'round the fire,
Stories told with heart's desire.
Under stars, so clear, so bright,
Winter's wonder paints the night.

Celestial Frost Kisses the Earth

Soft sparkles dance in twilight's glow,
A sparkling quilt upon the snow.
Whispers of joy in frosty air,
As laughter twirls without a care.

Candles flicker in windows bright,
Filling the world with warm delight.
Footprints trail where dreams take flight,
Underneath the stars so white.

Iridescent Patterns on a Glassy Lake

Waves shimmer with colors so bold,
Reflecting tales of warmth retold.
Children's laughter rings like bells,
Casting spells with magical swells.

Rowboats glide, beneath the sun,
Playing games, oh what fun!
Sunset paints with golden hue,
A canvas brushed in vibrant blue.

Glittering Veil over the Sleeping Fields

A blanket of white hugs the ground,
Serenity in silence found.
Stars peek through the evening mist,
Embraced in nature's gentle twist.

Fires crackle with a cheerful sound,
Gatherings pulse all around.
Hearts connect through stories shared,
In this magic, all are spared.

Ethereal Beauty of a Frigid Breath

Winds whisper secrets, crisp and sweet,
Gentle sighs of winter's beat.
Mittens used to catch the air,
Moments frozen, memories rare.

Icicles shine like diamonds bright,
As nature bathes in silver light.
Every breath a cloud of dreams,
In this wonder, life redeems.

Cold Sparkles

In the night, stars twinkle bright,
Snowflakes dance, pure delight.
Children laugh, voices cheer,
Holiday magic drawing near.

Lights aglow, the trees stand tall,
Parties echo, laughter's call.
Warmth of cocoa, sweet and rich,
Joy unwinds, we all enrich.

Gifts wrapped tight, with ribbons fair,
Excitement hangs in frosty air.
Together we gather, hearts ablaze,
Celebrating love in festive ways.

As the night fades, memories remain,
Cold sparkles of joy, we entertain.
In this season, all feel bright,
Embracing the warmth of pure delight.

Frosty Mirage in the Moonlight

Under the moon's soft, silvery glow,
Snow blankets the earth, soft and slow.
Carols sung, drifting through air,
Magic lingers everywhere.

Candles flicker, firelight glows,
Families gather, warmth bestows.
Cookies baked, sweet scent in the breeze,
Laughter wraps us, hearts at ease.

Icicles hang like jewels bright,
In this frosty mirage, pure delight.
Stories shared, bonds grow strong,
Moments cherished, where we belong.

As the night whispers, dreams take flight,
Guiding our hearts through deep of night.
In this season's hold, we unite,
With frosty mirage in moonlight.

Chilled Radiance

Snowflakes twirl in joyous dance,
Laughter rings in a winter's trance.
Twinkling lights adorn each tree,
A frosty cheer, so wild and free.

Warm cocoa hugs in gloved hands,
Fireplace crackles, soft demands.
Friends gather close, sharing delight,
In the heart of a winter night.

Glittering dreams in every eye,
Beneath the vast and starry sky.
Chilled radiance glows within,
As hearts ignite with festive spin.

A Glimpse of Crystal Light

Glimmering snow on the ground,
Frosty whispers all around.
Children's laughter fills the air,
Joyous spirit everywhere.

Sparkling dreams in the night sky,
As starry wishes drift on high.
Icicles hang like crystal chandeliers,
Glimpse of magic through the years.

Hushed the world, but hearts are loud,
Wrapped in love, a vibrant shroud.
Moments shared, a warm embrace,
In this festive, wondrous space.

Frosty Fantasy

Whispers of winter weave through trees,
Frosty kisses in the breeze.
Joyful songs spill from the heart,
As families gather, never apart.

Twinkling lights in the soft night,
A canvas painted with pure delight.
Snowmen rise with cheerful glee,
In this frosty fantasy.

Beneath the stars, a soft glow,
Magic unfolds as the cold winds blow.
Hearts unite, laughter and cheers,
Creating memories through the years.

Icicles as Stars

Icicles hang like stars of ice,
Nature's jewels, so cool and nice.
Underneath a moonlit sky,
Dreamers gaze as moments fly.

Children play in a winter's glow,
Building wonders in the snow.
Laughter rings, a sweet refrain,
In the shimmer of frosty rain.

Warmth of hearts, shining bright,
Wrapped in joy on this special night.
Icicles twinkle, softly hum,
A festive tune, a joyful drum.

Frigid Elegy

Snowflakes dance on cold winds,
Joyful laughter fills the air.
Bright lights twinkle in the night,
Hearts are warm and spirits fair.

Fires crackle in the hearth,
Sipping cocoa, warmth's embrace.
Families gather, stories told,
Love and peace in every space.

Songs of cheer fill up the streets,
Candles glow with golden light.
Hope is wrapped in every gift,
A festive spirit shines so bright.

Together we shall raise a glass,
To moments shared and memories dear.
As winter wraps us in its charm,
We celebrate with love and cheer.

Hushed Beneath Ice

Stillness blankets all the ground,
Stars reflect on frozen lakes.
Whispers ride the winter breeze,
No one stirs, no one wakes.

In this hush, our dreams take flight,
Sparkling frost like diamonds shine.
Underneath the tranquil night,
We find peace in love's design.

Laughter lingers in the air,
Voices dance on frosty breath.
Warmth ignites amidst the chill,
Life and joy conquer the death.

As the world around us sleeps,
We embrace this magic time.
With every moment that we share,
The festive spirit feels sublime.

Celestial Murmurs

Glistening stars like scattered jewels,
Whisper secrets from the skies.
Festive spirits in our hearts,
Inviting dreams as daylight dies.

Moonlight dances on the snow,
Casting shadows soft and bright.
We gather close, our hearts aglow,
Underneath the magical night.

Songs of laughter fill the air,
Echoed through the frosty trees.
Every moment shared is rare,
Carried gently on the breeze.

Together we embrace the spark,
Of friendship deep and love so true.
In celestial murmurs, we sing,
With every note, we welcome new.

Frosted Lanterns of Night

Glow of lanterns line the streets,
Casting warmth on chilly ground.
This festive night brings us together,
Joy and laughter all around.

Crisp air filled with scents so sweet,
Spices mingle, cheer abound.
Friends and family gather close,
In this bond, our hearts are found.

Winds of winter softly sing,
A lullaby of joy and peace.
Underneath the twinkling stars,
Our souls find solace and release.

Frosted lanterns shining bright,
Guide us through this festive night.
With every smile, with every cheer,
We celebrate this time of year.

Frosty Enchantment

Snowflakes dance in the air,
Sparkling whispers everywhere.
Children laugh, their cheeks aglow,
Joyful spirit in the snow.

Twinkling lights on every tree,
A celebration, wild and free.
Warmth of hearts as cold winds blow,
Frosty dreams in the moon's glow.

Diamond Dust Falling

Glistening facets fall around,
Nature's jewels adorn the ground.
Happiness blooms among the chill,
Magic moments time does still.

With every flake, a story spun,
Laughter mingles, joy begun.
The world transformed, a sight so bright,
Diamond dust beneath soft light.

Shards of Winter's Light

Crystal shards in the morning's gleam,
Reflecting beauty like a dream.
Sunrise kisses the frosted pines,
Whispers of gifts in nature's designs.

Gathered loved ones, spirits soar,
Winter's embrace, forever more.
In every glance, a warmth ignites,
Hope and cheer in winter's light.

Icicles' Melodic Lullaby

Icicles hang, a sparkling show,
Nature's music in the snow.
Gentle chimes as breezes play,
Melodies drift and dance away.

Fireside tales, laughter so bright,
Crackling warmth in the night.
Together we share this blissful sound,
In winter's arms, love is found.

Shimmering Chill of Dawn

In the morning's soft embrace,
A shimmer dances on the snow.
Laughter bubbles in the air,
As sunlight paints the world aglow.

Children dash with joy and glee,
Building dreams in frozen lands.
Hot cocoa warms our chilly hands,
Together here, as time expands.

The trees adorned with crystal lace,
A festival of winter's charms.
Each flake a tale of silent grace,
As nature lulls us in its arms.

Frosty Whispers

Whispers echo in the breeze,
As frosty patterns twirl and sway.
Joyful sings the merry trees,
In this winter wonderway.

Scarves wrap tight around our necks,
While twinkling lights begin to shine.
The night is filled with sweet effects,
Underneath the stars divine.

Hot pies cooling on the sill,
As cheerful voices fill the night.
Frosty air and hearts that thrill,
In this season's pure delight.

Glacial Elegance

Glistening like a diamond ring,
The world transforms with every flake.
Each breath a crystalline offering,
In this wonderland we wake.

Gather 'round the sparkling fire,
With tales that dance on winter's breath.
Our spirits high with pure desire,
To celebrate while skies are deft.

Frost-kissed branches gently sway,
As night wraps all in silver hue.
Glacial elegance holds sway,
In every dream that's born anew.

A Glint of Frost

A glint of frost upon the ground,
Whispers secrets of the night.
With every step, the joy is found,
As morning breaks to pure delight.

Snowflakes twirl like playful sprites,
Dancing in a waltz of grace.
The world adorned in snowy whites,
A canvas pure, a soft embrace.

With laughter echoing so bright,
We share the warmth of love and cheer.
In this season's sparkling light,
Festivity wraps us ever near.

Glistening Twilight

The sky paints hues of gold,
As laughter fills the air,
Children dance, a joyful sight,
With twinkling lights everywhere.

Crisp leaves crunch beneath our feet,
As friends gather near the fire,
Stories told, old and new,
Hearts warm with the night's desire.

Candles flicker, shadows play,
Underneath the starry dome,
Every moment feels so bright,
In this place, we find our home.

So raise a glass, let voices sing,
To love and joy, our spirits soar,
In this glistening twilight world,
Together, we ask for nothing more.

Sparkling Shadows of Winter

Snowflakes dance on winter's breath,
Covering the ground so white,
In the hush of falling night,
Whispers of the season's depth.

Fires crackle, warm and bright,
Stories shared by flickering glow,
Outside, the chilly winds do blow,
While inside, hearts feel the light.

Glittering decorations gleam,
Adorning every joyful space,
In this season, we find grace,
As dreams awaken from a dream.

Together we raise our cheer,
With cookies, laughter, songs we sing,
In the sparkling shadows, we cling,
To memories that bring us near.

The Frost's Gentle Touch

A blanket woven pure and white,
Each branch kissed with frosty grace,
Nature dons a quiet lace,
Bringing magic to the night.

Children's laughter floats like song,
As snowballs fly, a frosty fight,
Underneath the pale moonlight,
Their joy is where we all belong.

The warmth of cocoa in our hands,
As we gather, share our cheer,
In the crispness, love feels near,
Creating memories like soft bands.

So let the frost weave through our hearts,
With every twinkle in the sky,
In this shimmering lullaby,
The gentle touch of winter starts.

Chasing Icicle Dreams

Icicles hang like crystal chimes,
Reflecting sunlight in the morn,
Around us, winter's beauty forms,
A canvas painted with frost's rhymes.

Sleds glide down the hills with glee,
Cheers echo through the frosty air,
Every moment holds a dare,
As we chase dreams, wild and free.

Fires crackle, shadows dance,
With loved ones close, the world feels bright,
In this wonderland of light,
We dive into the season's trance.

So let us play, let laughter ring,
With every snowflake that we catch,
In our hearts, we attach,
To frosty joy, the joy of spring.

Chilling Splendor

Snowflakes dance in the crisp night air,
Laughter rings out, joy everywhere.
Bright lights twinkle, a festive glow,
Warm hearts embrace the cold below.

Children's voices, pure delight,
Singing carols, spirits bright.
A cozy fire crackles near,
Hot cocoa warms, the time is here.

Mittens snug, and cheeks aglow,
Gathered close, friends all in tow.
Together we share, stories unfold,
Creating memories, treasures to hold.

As winter blankets the world in white,
The chilling splendor feels just right.
Celebrations bloom with each new day,
In this frosty town, we laugh and play.

Fragments of Ice-Bound Light

Icicles hang like delicate art,
Reflecting the warmth of each loving heart.
Winter's breath whispers soft and clear,
In this moment, we feel no fear.

Colorful lights twinkle in pairs,
Embracing the moon with shimmering flares.
Children skate on the frozen lake,
While joyful laughter delights the wake.

Each snowflake tells a tale anew,
Of dreams that sparkle and wishes true.
Fragments of light in the evening's hold,
A sight of beauty, a sight to behold.

Together we gather, share in the night,
With hearts as one, our spirits take flight.
Fragments of joy in our festive cheer,
In this wonderland, the magic's here.

Whispering Frost

Whispering frost on the window panes,
Nature's secrets in soft refrains.
Chills in the air spark playful delight,
As we feast and revel through the night.

Beneath the stars, our laughter soars,
Echoing sweetly past open doors.
Smiles are shared, as stories unfold,
In warm embraces, love's joys are told.

Bonfires crackle, the warmth we crave,
Dancing shadows, the spirits we save.
Every moment wrapped in pure bliss,
A whispered promise, a gentle kiss.

Frosty patterns weave tales we share,
Of friendships cherished, beyond compare.
Whispering frost in this magic light,
Holds us close on this wondrous night.

Glistening Dreams of Winter

Glistening dreams in the pale moonlight,
Snow-covered branches, a beautiful sight.
A symphony whispers through the pines,
Echoing secrets in playful lines.

Crisp air twirls the laughter around,
Joyous echoes in the frosty ground.
Children pile snow in a cozy hug,
While cocoa warms hearts like a snug drug.

Each flake a wish, each twinkle a spark,
Together we gather in the brightening dark.
Stories like snowflakes drift and play,
In glistening dreams, we find our way.

As winter paints every corner with glee,
We treasure the moments, just you and me.
Glistening dreams dance through the air,
In this festive wonder, love's everywhere.

Frosted Dreams Unfurled

In winter's light, the snowflakes dance,
Children's laughter, a joyful chance.
Glistening trees, adorned with cheer,
Frosted dreams draw loved ones near.

Warmth of cocoa, splashes of red,
Whispers of stories, sweetly spread.
Fireplace crackles, shadows sway,
In this festive night, we find our way.

Twinkling lights in every sight,
Filling the hearts with pure delight.
Gifts wrapped tightly, bows of gold,
Moments like these are worth more than gold.

Eager songs fill the chilly air,
Bells ring out, a signal rare.
Frosted dreams, together we mold,
In this winter wonder, love unfolds.

Ethereal Winter's Embrace

Softly falls the whispering snow,
Blanketing the earth in glow.
Icicles gleam like crystal prisms,
Nature's art in proud rhythms.

Children build their castles tall,
With laughter echoing through it all.
Mittens warming tiny hands,
Ethereal joy that never lands.

Songs of carols fill the air,
Spreading warmth, each note a prayer.
Stars above begin to shine,
A festive spirit, truly divine.

With each heart, the magic grows,
In winter's embrace, love overflows.
Gathered close, the world feels right,
Under the moon's gentle light.

Morning's Crystal Tapestry

Awake to frost, the world's anew,
A crystal tapestry, glistening dew.
Morning sun ignites the skies,
Painting warmth in every rise.

Footprints crunch on the fresh white snow,
A playful chase as the cold winds blow.
Warm breakfast scents fill the air,
In this cozy home, we share.

Stockings hung by the fire's glow,
Chiming laughter weaves like a bow.
Holding hands, we dance with glee,
Morning's crystal, wild and free.

Every hug, a cherished treasure,
Moments woven beyond all measure.
In life's tapestry, colors blend,
A festive journey that will never end.

Silvered Breath of Air

The world shimmers in silvered light,
A breath of air, crisp and bright.
Candles flicker, their flames so bold,
Stories shared, each moment told.

Glistening pathways, snowflakes twirl,
In the magic of winter's whirl.
Sleigh bells ring through joy and mirth,
Celebrating the season's worth.

Hearts aglow, we raise our cheer,
With every gathering, love draws near.
Silvered breath upon the night,
Together, we dance in pure delight.

Gifts of kindness, wrapped with care,
In every smile, we breathe a prayer.
This festive season, hand in hand,
In each warm heart, forever stand.

A Glimmer of Hope in Winter's Grasp

A fire crackles in the night,
As snowflakes dance in silver light.
Voices laugh and spirits soar,
In hearth's warm glow, we yearn for more.

The world adorned in crystal white,
Each breath a cloud, a pure delight.
Together friends, our hearts aglow,
In winter's grasp, love's warmth will grow.

The stars above, a sparkling show,
A glimmer caught, where dreams can flow.
With every cheer, the year renews,
In festive joy, we chase our blues.

With cocoa sweet and stories shared,
A tapestry of love declared.
Through winter's chill, our bond will clasp,
A glimmer of hope in winter's grasp.

Morning's Hush: Nature's Glitter

In morning hush, the world awakes,
With gentle light that softly breaks.
A twinkle rests on every tree,
Nature's glitter, wild and free.

Frozen branches, sparkling bright,
Hues of gold in soft daylight.
Each step a crunch, a joyous sound,
In winter's magic, peace is found.

The air is crisp, the sky so clear,
With every breath, joy draws near.
A symphony of sights and sounds,
In morning's hush, our spirit bounds.

We gather close, with hearts in tow,
Under the spell of winter's show.
In this embrace, the world feels right,
As morning's hush holds pure delight.

Hues of Ice Beneath Morning's Gaze

Beneath the sun, a world so bright,
Hues of ice catch morning's light.
Reflections dance in colors bold,
A tapestry of dreams unfolds.

With every step, we trace the glint,
In wonderland, where hearts can mint.
The laughter shared, a joyful tease,
In frosted air, our minds find ease.

Snowflakes tumble with playful grace,
Nature's canvas, a soft embrace.
We twirl and spin, our spirits high,
While winter whispers a lullaby.

In every flake, a story spun,
Of chilly days, yet filled with fun.
With hues of ice, we find our gaze,
In winter's glow, we sing its praise.

Transparent Wonders of the Wintry World

Through frosty panes, the world is seen,
Transparent wonders, fresh and clean.
Icicles dangle, shimmering bright,
A spell of joy in purest sight.

The pathways gleam where footprints tread,
Each step a spark, where none may dread.
With rosy cheeks and laughter shared,
In this cold bliss, we're all prepared.

A quilt of snow, so soft and white,
As sunbeams dance in pure delight.
With joyous hearts, we twine and weave,
In winter's charm, we truly believe.

So gather 'round, let voices blend,
In winter's cheer, our hearts extend.
With brilliant sights and spirits swirled,
We celebrate this wintry world.

Glowed Reflections of a Winter's Heart

In the glow of twilight's embrace,
Laughter dances, a warm, bright trace.
Children's giggles fill the frosty air,
As joy sparkles, lighting everywhere.

Candles flicker, casting spells so bright,
Gentle whispers paint the starry night.
Warm drinks cradle in hands so tight,
Hearts entwined, a pure festive sight.

Snowflakes twirl in the crisp, cool breeze,
Nature's chorus sways with such ease.
Each fleeting moment, a treasure we keep,
In winter's heart, our memories leap.

With every glow, a promise unfolds,
In the warmth of love, true happiness molds.
Together we gather, our spirits ignite,
In the glow of reflections, a winter's delight.

Celestial Crystals in Nature's Gallery

Glistening crystals adorn each tree,
Nature's jewels, so wild and free.
Underneath the moon's soft, silver light,
The world transformed into purest white.

Whispers of magic float on the breeze,
With every sparkle, the heart finds ease.
Children chase shadows, their laughter a bell,
In this gallery, where wonders dwell.

Frosted branches, a delicate lace,
Moments cherished, a warm embrace.
As starlight twinkles, dreams take flight,
Celebration weaves through this beautiful night.

In every flake, a story to share,
Nature's brilliance beyond compare.
Together beneath this celestial dome,
In nature's gallery, we find our home.

Lacy Patterns on the Boughs

Lacy patterns weave through every tree,
A tapestry of wonder for all to see.
Branches embrace their frosty attire,
Swaying gently as if to inspire.

Glittering elegance, nature's own art,
Inviting the spirit, it warms the heart.
Children wrap, their laughter take flight,
In every flurry, the joys of the night.

Crisp air sparkles, the ground brushed with white,
As dreams awaken in the soft moonlight.
Each flake a whisper, a festive cheer,
Lacy patterns beckon, bringing us near.

Under the twilight, as shadows play,
We gather together to sing and sway.
In nature's design, we lose track of time,
Lacy patterns remind us, life is sublime.

Night's Tapestry of Frosted Stars

Underneath the quilt of night's embrace,
Frosted stars glimmer, a magical space.
With every twinkle, our spirits arise,
Painting the world with wonder and skies.

Songs of the night in harmony blend,
As laughter and joy become the trend.
Gathered together, we hold dear the light,
In this tapestry woven so bright.

Candles glow, casting shadows that dance,
In merriment, we take a chance.
Frosted whispers caress the dark,
Starlit memories ignite a spark.

As the night deepens, hearts intertwine,
In this festive glow, we truly shine.
Nature rejoices in the calm of the stars,
Night's beauty wraps us, forever ours.

Ephemeral Frost Shapes

In the dawn's tender glow,
Frost laces every branch,
Whispers of joy dance light,
Nature's artwork at a glance.

Snowflakes twirl in the sun,
Glittering like tiny stars,
Children laugh, hearts run free,
Chasing dreams from near to far.

Together we build our dreams,
Snowmen tall with warm, bright scarves,
In a world adorned in white,
Festive cheer forever carves.

With each cup of cocoa shared,
Warmth spreads like a lovely song,
Hearts unite in frosty fun,
Where we all feel we belong.

Glacial Harmony

Icicles shimmer, softly sway,
Beneath the pale moon's embrace,
The world glistens, hushed and bright,
A peaceful, festive space.

Footprints crunch on the pathway,
Songs of the season unfold,
Voices echo, warm and light,
Tales of wonder retold.

Candles flicker in the night,
As laughter fills the air,
We gather close, hearts aglow,
In a moment rare and fair.

From feasting on sweet delights,
To sharing the joys we have,
Each memory, a spark divine,
In our hearts, forever save.

Translucent Winter Hope

Beneath the barren branches,
Hope glimmers like morning dew,
Each sparkle tells a secret,
Of dreams that will soon come true.

Winter whispers softly,
In each flake that starts to fall,
Each one a wish, a promise,
For joy to blanket all.

Gathered 'round the fire's glow,
Voices rise in harmony,
Sharing tales of love and light,
Filling hearts with glee.

Through frosty trails we wander,
With laughter trailing behind,
In this place of fleeting time,
Our spirits intertwined.

Crystalized Morning's Echo

Morning breaks with crystal light,
Casting shadows, bright and clear,
A world transformed, a canvas white,
Filled with warmth and holiday cheer.

Silence wraps the sleeping earth,
As snowflakes swirl in twinkling flight,
Each tiny flake a gift of mirth,
Painting a wonderland at night.

Joyful hearts come alive,
Spirits lift with joyous song,
In this season of our dreams,
Where we all feel we belong.

Through every echoing laugh,
And every twinkling light displayed,
Together we weave, side by side,
A tapestry of memories made.

Shimmering Winter's Breath

Snowflakes dance in joyful flight,
Twinkling stars adorn the night.
Laughter echoes, warm and bright,
Embracing all in pure delight.

Warmth of fire, stories share,
Wrapping hearts in loving care.
Mirthful songs fill icy air,
Togetherness beyond compare.

Pine trees gleam with ribbons bold,
Each moment cherished, stories told.
Winter's charm, a sight to hold,
A tapestry of memories gold.

Here we gather, joy embraced,
In this season, love is placed.
With every heart, a smile traced,
Shimmering winter, life interlaced.

Frosty Reflections

Morning light on frosted glass,
Glistening echoes of the past.
In each breath, the moments pass,
As friendships bloom, shadows cast.

Children's laughter, pure and free,
Creating snowmen, joy's decree.
With every fall, a sense of glee,
Frosty air, like harmony.

Crystals hanging, nature's art,
A season's magic warms the heart.
When winter plays its playful part,
Together, we'll never part.

In twilight's glow, a magic scene,
Where joy and wonder reign as queen.
Frosty reflections, bright and keen,
A festive world, like a dream.

Glistening Nightfall

Lights above like scattered gems,
Dancing shadows, joy begins.
Winter's hush, a soft diadem,
Whispers of peace, the night transcends.

Carols sung by crackling flames,
Frosty air, with laughter claims.
Beneath the stars, we call their names,
In glistening night, love inflames.

White blankets soft on ground below,
Every step brings smiles aglow.
Memories made in the evening's flow,
In this festive space, we grow.

The moonlit paths, so bright and clear,
Celebrate moments, far and near.
In each heartbeat, festive cheer,
Glistening nightfall, winter's dear.

Enigmatic Chills

Whispers ride the frosty breeze,
Secrets kept among the trees.
Every flake, a tale to tease,
In winter's grasp, the heart's unease.

Mysterious night with stars aligned,
Echoes of the past combined.
Glimmers of warmth in all we find,
In this chill, our souls unwind.

Moonbeams weaving through the pines,
Shimmering hope that intertwines.
With friends beside, the joy defines,
In enigmatic chills, love shines.

So gather close, let laughter swell,
In the magic of this spell.
With every heartbeat, all is well,
In winter's heart, our stories tell.

Captivated by Cold

The air is crisp, a joyous thrill,
Laughter dances, hearts to fill.
Snowflakes swirl like joyful dreams,
In this wonderland, nothing seems.

Friends gather 'round with cups in hand,
Stories shared in this frosty land.
Firelight flickers, warmth does glow,
Outside the chill, inside the flow.

Laughter peals through winter's night,
Every face a spark of light.
The world aglow, a festive sight,
Captivated by cold, hearts take flight.

Together we sing, our voices soar,
Finding magic in winter's lore.
Each moment savored, pure delight,
Captivated by cold, a cherished night.

Luminous Fragments of Chill

Glittering snowflakes paint the ground,
In the hush, sweet joy is found.
Lanterns glow, a warm embrace,
Luminous fragments fill the space.

Cheerful shouts and playful games,
Echo through the winter flames.
Bundled tight in scarves and hats,
Dancing with the cheerful cats.

Under stars, the laughter swells,
Each moment like a magic spell.
Frosty breath in the starry night,
Luminous fragments, pure delight.

With every cheer, the cold retreats,
As hearts grow warm in joyful beats.
Together here, the world feels bright,
Luminous fragments of chill, our light.

Charmed by Frost

Morning breaks with silver hues,
Frosted fields, a charming muse.
Children giggle, running free,
Charmed by frost, like magic spree.

Grateful hearts, we come alive,
In every flake, our spirits thrive.
Hot cocoa warms each smiling face,
In this frosty, playful space.

Gathering 'round the tree aglow,
Stories shared in the evening's flow.
Memories made with joy and cheer,
Charmed by frost, we hold most dear.

As the day fades, lights twinkle bright,
Friendships cherished, love takes flight.
In the stillness, we softly boast,
Of the magic found, charming frost.

Frosted Kisses at Dawn

The dawn awakens with tender grace,
Frosted kisses in every place.
Sunrise glitters, a warm embrace,
Winter's beauty we all chase.

Whispers of joy in the chilly air,
Frosty mornings, a moment rare.
Bundled tight in glittering white,
Frosted kisses, hearts feel light.

The world aglow in softest tones,
With every step, the winter moans.
Nature beckons, come and play,
Frosted kisses greet the day.

Together we laugh, our spirits bright,
In frosted moments, pure delight.
As the sun rises, love inspires,
Frosted kisses, warm fires.

Whispers of Winter's Glimmer

Snowflakes dance in the bright moonlight,
Bells that jingle, hearts take flight.
Warm fires crackle, voices cheer,
Together we gather, love drawing near.

Laughter echoes through the air,
Scents of pine and spice to share.
Candles flicker, spirits rise,
Magic twinkles in joyful eyes.

Sleds rush down the sparkling hill,
Chilled fingers clutch a cup to fill.
Songs of old fill the night,
Whispers of warmth, pure delight.

As stars blanket our cozy town,
We wear our smiles, no trace of frown.
In this wonder, time stands still,
Whispers of joy, our hearts to thrill.

Crystal Dreams on a Chilly Dawn

Morning breaks with a soft embrace,
Frosted whispers, nature's grace.
Birds awaken with a cheerful song,
In this freshness, we all belong.

Glistening branches, a shining sight,
Sunlight dances, pure delight.
A hush falls over the waking land,
Winter's beauty, so gently planned.

Coffee brews with an earthy cheer,
Gathering friends, bringing near.
Steaming mugs and warm, sweet treats,
Laughter mingles; this joy repeats.

Each moment savored, joy refined,
In crystal dreams, our hearts aligned.
With chilly breezes, we feel the glow,
Together in warmth, our spirits flow.

Shimmering Silence in the Stillness

In the hush of a winter's night,
Stars above shine brilliantly bright.
Snow blankets all, soft and deep,
In this silence, our hearts will leap.

Footprints venture in the snow,
Guiding paths where warm fires glow.
Voices echo in the chilly air,
With every whisper, magic we share.

Cocoa flowing in festive mugs,
All around, cheerful shrugs.
Conversations dance like sparkled lights,
We embrace the warmth of winter nights.

In this stillness, dreams take flight,
Together we revel in pure delight.
Shimmering futures twinkle ahead,
In the snowy silence, our hearts are fed.

Frosted Petals in Morning Light

Morning glows with a gentle sheen,
Frosted petals, a dazzling scene.
Nature awakens, colors blaze,
In this splendor, we all praise.

Delicate blooms under icy kiss,
Every petal whispers bliss.
Joy abounds in gardens bright,
Frosted beauty, pure delight.

Birds flutter with melodious cheer,
Each soft note brings loved ones near.
In every corner, laughter plays,
Frosted petals in winter's gaze.

As sunlight bathes the world in gold,
Stories of love and warmth unfold.
With every moment, let's make it right,
Embracing life in morning light.

Radiant Jewels on the Frozen Ground

Glistening diamonds in the snow,
Nature's treasure, a lovely show.
Twinkling colors, warm and bright,
Hearts are lifted in pure delight.

Children giggle, joy abounds,
In this wonderland, beauty surrounds.
Laughter echoes, spirits soar,
Radiant jewels, we all adore.

Frosty breath dances in the air,
Playful moments, without a care.
Whispers of magic, softly spun,
A festive world, for everyone.

Gathered together, friends so dear,
Wishing warmth and festive cheer.
As the stars twinkle from above,
We celebrate with joy and love.

Magic in the Icy Air

Breathe in the magic, chill and bright,
Icicles sparkling, a wondrous sight.
Winds of laughter swirl and play,
Dancing shadows of the day.

Snowflakes twirl like little sprites,
Flickering candles on winter nights.
Each moment filled with joyful bliss,
A festive smile, a winter kiss.

Ornaments shining on the trees,
Rustling branches in the breeze.
Muffled giggles, the thrill of the chase,
In the frosty air, we find our place.

Hearts are glowing, senses awake,
Memories made, no chance to fake.
Wonders abound, as spirits climb,
Magic in the icy air, sublime.

Glinting Traces of a Hidden Spell

Footprints sparkle on the snowy lane,
Each a story, a joyful refrain.
Stars above with a shimmering glow,
Hints of magic in the frosty flow.

Whispers of secrets, the night reveals,
Glinting traces, the heart feels.
Moments captured, frozen in time,
A magical dance, a festive rhyme.

Frosted whispers call us near,
Sparks of joy, both calm and clear.
Days filled with warmth, laughter, and song,
In this wonder, we all belong.

Wonders unfold with each gentle breath,
A tapestry woven, defying death.
Life and laughter, forever dwell,
In the glinting traces of a hidden spell.

Chime of Frost on a Quiet Path

Chimes of frost sing through the trees,
A melody carried on the breeze.
Each step echoes, soft and low,
In a wonderland wrapped in snow.

Whispers of winter grace the way,
Glittering fields where children play.
Every glimmer holds a sweet refrain,
In this festive, enchanted domain.

Footprints etched in a crystal dream,
Memories gathered like a warm stream.
Wonders clinging to every bough,
Chime of frost, we cherish now.

As laughter mingles with the cold,
Stories of warmth and joy unfold.
Together we walk, as spirits align,
In the chime of frost, the world is fine.

Frost's Brush: Nature's Delicate Art

In early morn, the world awakes,
With glittering jewels on silent lakes.
A touch of white on branches sway,
As nature dons her bright ballet.

The sun peeks through, a golden thread,
Painting dreams where shadows tread.
With laughter twinkling in the air,
Joyful whispers everywhere.

Children dance in winter's cheer,
Creating trails with festive gear.
Their voices rise, a lively song,
With every step, they dance along.

The world adorned in frosty lace,
A magic spell in every place.
Together, hearts embrace the day,
As winter's brush leads the way.

Chilling Brilliance on Forgotten Leaves

Amidst the trees, a secret glows,
Chilling brilliance in icy flows.
Leaves once bright, now frozen still,
Whispers of nature, a breath, a thrill.

Each step crumbles the shimm'ring ground,
A festive echo, a joyful sound.
With every breath, the world aglow,
Embracing winter's gentle show.

Soft laughter dances on the breeze,
Tickling branches, rustling leaves.
A tapestry of white and blue,
In nature's art, fresh and new.

Beneath the sky, so vast, so bright,
November's chill, a pure delight.
In every flake, a story spun,
Together, we share in winter's fun.

The Ice-Kissed Symphony of Solitude

In tranquil woods, the silence reigns,
An ice-kissed symphony remains.
Each drop of frost, a note in tune,
Reflects the silver light of moon.

The world slows down; the heart takes flight,
Embraced by winter's soft, pure light.
Whispers of peace in every flake,
Where solitude knows no heartache.

Beneath the glimmer, a secret lies,
Nature's rhythm, a sweet surprise.
With every breath, the air feels new,
A moment shared between us two.

As branches sway, a gentle dance,
In frost's embrace, we take our chance.
Together we celebrate this night,
In his quiet symphony of light.

Resplendent Crystals in the Fading Light

As dusk descends with gentle grace,
Resplendent crystals light the space.
Fragile wonders, shining bright,
In the embrace of fading light.

Twinkling dreams on every glance,
Invite us all to join the dance.
With laughter echoing through the air,
We revel in the joy we share.

The stars peek out, a festive cheer,
Wrapped in warmth, drawing us near.
While shadows play on winter's skin,
A dance begins, let joy begin.

In this moment, we find our part,
A celebration woven with heart.
With every breath, our spirits soar,
As resplendent crystals, we adore.

Glacial Dances in the Sun's Embrace

Under the sun, where ice does gleam,
Laughter rings out, like a joyous dream.
Snowflakes twirl in a frosty ballet,
Nature's orchestra plays on display.

Children giggle, their cheeks aglow,
Chasing the sparkles in the crisp snow.
Every moment shines, a treasure trove,
In this winter wonderland, we rove.

Warm cups of cocoa in gloved hands tight,
Radiant sunsets, a stunning sight.
Folks gather 'round, their spirits lifted,
In glacial strains, our hearts are gifted.

Beneath the stars, a soft glow spreads,
Fires burn bright, as night gently threads.
With songs and stories, we dance along,
In the sun's embrace, we found our song.

Enchanted Ice: A Silver Poem

In the stillness, where whispers flit,
Crystals dance softly, in twilight lit.
Silver glimmers on every face,
A magic spell in this frozen place.

Frosted branches sway with ease,
As the gentle winter winds tease.
Songs of joy weave through the air,
Glistening wonders, a loving affair.

Each step crunches, a sweet refrain,
Echoes of laughter, a soft champagne.
Under the moon, our spirits soar,
In enchanted ice, we crave for more.

Joyous hearts reflect the night,
With dreams aglow in soft starlight.
Together we weave our stories bright,
In the shimmering world, pure delight.

Luminous Crystals Under Twilight Skies

Twilight whispers, the sky alight,
Crystals shimmer in the gentle night.
Stars twinkle dreams in our hopeful gaze,
Crafting a world where our hearts blaze.

In the stillness, magic we find,
With every moment, our souls aligned.
Snowflakes twirling like soft ballet,
As laughter joins in, a bright array.

Luminous paths lead us anew,
Through glistening realms in varying hue.
Friendship's warmth, a radiant glow,
In this winter's embrace, love will flow.

We gather close as music swells,
The rhythm of joy, in our hearts dwells.
Under twilight's watch, we come alive,
In shimmering crystals, our spirits thrive.

Breath of Winter's Glistening Touch

Winter breathes softly, a gentle sigh,
A touch of frost as the night drifts by.
Snowflakes flutter like delicate dreams,
Painting the world in celestial beams.

Laughter spills out, a joyous parade,
In this frosty realm where memories fade.
Children play, their cheeks rosy bright,
As the stars twinkle in velvety night.

Gift-wrapped whispers float on the breeze,
With every twirl, our worries cease.
The beauty of winter, a cherished friend,
In glistening moments, our hearts mend.

Around the fire, tales intertwine,
With mugs of warmth, our spirits align.
In winter's embrace, we find our place,
The breath of glistening touch, pure grace.

Frozen Ballerinas of the Night

Beneath the stars, twinkling bright,
Ballerinas spin in the night.
Their whispers drift on frosty air,
A magical charm, beyond compare.

Dressed in white, they dance with grace,
Each movement brings a frozen embrace.
In the moonlight, they glide so free,
Creating a symphony of glee.

With every leap, the crystals glow,
A shimmering stage, a world below.
Echoes of laughter fill the sky,
As winter's wonder dances by.

A jubilant show of frosty delight,
Ballerinas shine in the cool moonlight.
In the enchanting night, hearts take flight,
Frozen dreams brought to life, in sight.

A Dance on Glinting Crystals

Underneath the starry sheen,
Glinting crystals, pure and clean.
With every step, the world awakes,
In their dance, the stillness breaks.

Around the trees, they twirl and sway,
Creating magic, come what may.
The night is filled with joyful glee,
As nature sings its harmony.

Laughter echoes through the land,
A festive spirit, hand in hand.
Clad in frost, they leap so high,
Embracing dreams that touch the sky.

Each twinkle brings a spark of light,
A wondrous scene, so pure and bright.
Together, they weave a tale so clear,
Of glinting crystals and holiday cheer.

Frosted Serenity

In the hush of winter's night,
Frosted beauty, pure delight.
Gentle whispers glide on air,
Creating peace, beyond compare.

Lands adorned in icy lace,
Nature's magic, a soft embrace.
Snowflakes dance in twinkling beams,
Filling hearts with silvery dreams.

Beneath the trees, the shadows play,
A tranquil scene, where children stray.
With sparkling eyes, they chase the light,
In a world of frosted serenity, bright.

The festive joy of winter's grace,
Unravels time in this sacred space.
As silence wraps the world so tight,
In frosted bands, we find delight.

Enchanted by Ice

In the realm of glistening frost,
The beauty of winter never lost.
With every flake, the earth does glow,
An enchanted world, basked in snow.

Icicles hang like crystal dreams,
Reflecting the sun's gentle beams.
The air is filled with splendid cheer,
As laughter dances, warm and near.

Around the fire, stories entwine,
Hearts alight with joy divine.
In every moment, magic is spun,
United in warmth, we're never done.

The night unfolds with stars so bright,
Enchanted by ice, we share the light.
In this festive frost, we find our place,
In winter's embrace, we feel the grace.

Radiant Icicles

Icicles hanging, gleaming bright,
Reflecting colors in the light.
A winter dance, so crisp and clear,
Joyful whispers fill the air.

Children laughing, sleds in tow,
Every hill a place to go.
Snowflakes twirl in playful flight,
A world transformed, a pure delight.

Warm mugs steaming, fires aglow,
Stories shared as embers flow.
Under stars, a blanket's spread,
In this wonder, hearts are fed.

In these moments, time stands still,
With every breath, a magic thrill.
Radiant icicles, shining bright,
Celebrate the winter night.

Glittering Veils of Winter

Veils of snow on branches lay,
Sparkling softly in the day.
Nature's art in purest form,
A crystal world where dreams are born.

The air is filled with joyful sound,
As laughter echoes all around.
Children playing, hearts so free,
Wrapped in winter's harmony.

Twinkling lights adorn each home,
Guiding warmth through frosty dome.
Gathered close, we sing with glee,
Sharing love and memories.

In this season of pure delight,
Glittering veils shine ever bright.
Together we embrace the chill,
With hearts that dance and spirits thrill.

Whispered Glimmer

Whispers of glimmer, soft and near,
In the air, a sense of cheer.
Candles flicker, warmth begins,
Tales of wonder on winter winds.

Beneath the trees with branches bare,
Friends and family gather there.
Snowflakes fall like gentle sighs,
Underneath the starlit skies.

Hot cocoa shared, sweet and divine,
Fingers warmed on mugs entwined.
In each laugh, a spark of light,
Creating magic in the night.

With whispered glimmers all around,
Joy and peace are truly found.
In this moment, hearts align,
As winter's jewels brightly shine.

Celestial Frost Patterns

Frost patterns dance upon the glass,
Nature's artwork, time does pass.
Each design, a story spun,
Celestial magic, gifted fun.

Underneath the pale moon's glow,
Footprints trace where lovers go.
Hand in hand, with whispers sweet,
In winter's embrace, our souls meet.

Warm fires crackle, stories flow,
As soft winds sing, and embers glow.
Families gather, share their dreams,
In this wonder, love redeems.

Celestial frost, a silvery lace,
Adorning every open space.
With each breath, the chill feels right,
In perfect peace, we savor night.